TOP OF THE FOOD CHAIN

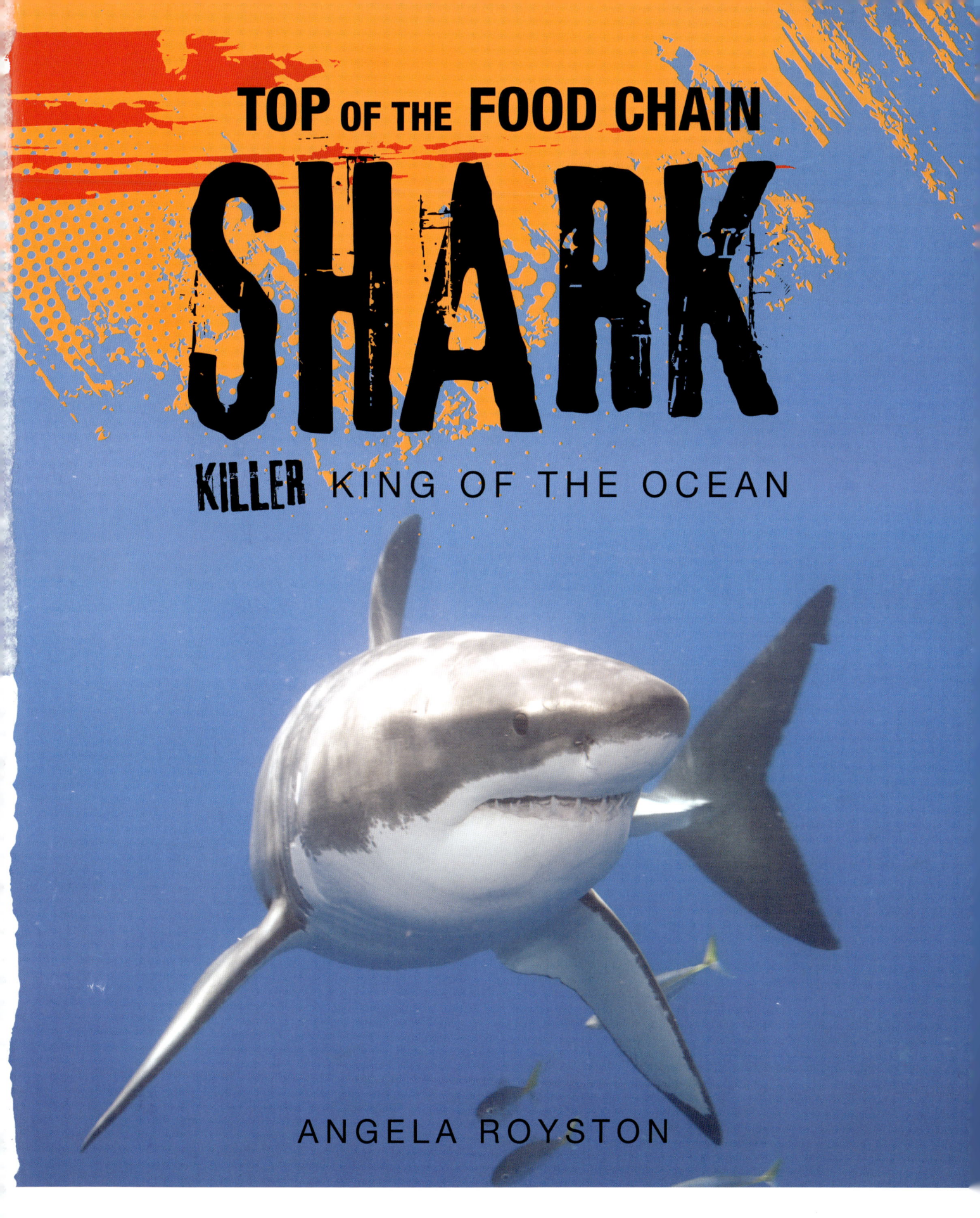

SHARK

KILLER KING OF THE OCEAN

ANGELA ROYSTON

raintree
a Capstone company — publishers for children

Raintree is an imprint of Capstone Global Library Limited, a company incorporated in England and Wales having its registered office at 264 Banbury Road, Oxford, OX2 7DY – Registered company number: 6695582

www.raintree.co.uk
myorders@raintree.co.uk

Text © Capstone Global Library Limited 2020
The moral rights of the proprietor have been asserted.

All rights reserved. No part of this publication may be reproduced in any form or by any means (including photocopying or storing it in any medium by electronic means and whether or not transiently or incidentally to some other use of this publication) without the written permission of the copyright owner, except in accordance with the provisions of the Copyright, Designs and Patents Act 1988 or under the terms of a licence issued by the Copyright Licensing Agency, Barnard's Inn, 86 Fetter Lane, London, EC4A 1EN (www.cla.co.uk). Applications for the copyright owner's written permission should be addressed to the publisher.

Produced for Raintree by Calcium Creative Ltd
Editor for Calcium Creative Ltd: Sarah Eason
Designers: Paul Myerscough and Keith Williams
Original illustrations © Capstone Global Library Limited 2020
Production by Katy LaVigne
Originated by Capstone Global Library Ltd
Printed and bound in India

ISBN 978 1 4747 7796 4 (hardback)
ISBN 978 1 4747 7802 2 (paperback)

British Library Cataloguing in Publication Data
A full catalogue record for this book is available from the British Library.

Acknowledgements
We would like to thank the following for permission to reproduce photographs: Shutterstock: 7, A Cotton Photo 11b, Jim Agronick 1, 9, 17, Willyam Bradberry 4, 28, Rich Carey 13, Mark Doherty 23, Igor Dutina 19r, FAUP 6, 12, Natali Glado 27b, Greg Amptman's Undersea Discoveries 16b, 18, Hainaultphoto 27c, K. L. Kohn 29, Peter Leahy 5, MJ007 25r, Natursports 15t, 26, I. Pilon 24b, Nastya Pirieva 16t, 19l, Sailorr 20, Ian Scott 8, 21, David P Stephens cover, 25l, Stubblefield Photography 15c, Teguh Tirtaputra 22, UROSR 11t, Dray van Beeck 14.

Every effort has been made to contact copyright holders of material reproduced in this book. Any omissions will be rectified in subsequent printings if notice is given to the publisher.

All the internet addresses (URLs) given in this book were valid at the time of going to press. However, due to the dynamic nature of the internet, some addresses may have changed, or sites may have changed or ceased to exist since publication. While the author and publisher regret any inconvenience this may cause readers, no responsibility for any such changes can be accepted by either the author or the publisher.

Suffolk Libraries	
30127 08709104 2	
Askews & Holts	Oct-2019
J597.3	£12.99

CONTENTS

Ocean king 4
Meet the sharks 6
Top predator 8
Shark attack 10
Streamlining 12
Fantastic fins 14
Killer teeth 16
Amazing smell 18
Special eyesight 20
Other senses 22
Great survivor 24
Shark dangers 26
No more sharks? 28
Glossary 30
Find out more 31
Index 32

OCEAN KING

Sharks live in the world's oceans, the largest habitat on Earth. They stay mainly in the shallow waters around the continents. Most sea creatures live in shallow water near the coast, so this is where sharks hunt for food.

Sharks are at the top of many food chains. These fierce predators hunt fish and other sea animals, which feed on smaller fish or shellfish. Plankton is at the bottom of most ocean food chains. Plankton is a mass of tiny sea animals and plants, which float on the ocean surface. Each animal in a food chain is linked to the animals and plants below it.

These three whitetip reef sharks are prowling around a reef in the Pacific Ocean. Danger is never far away for the fish that live on the reef.

LINKS IN THE FOOD CHAIN

Whitetip reef sharks lurk around coral reefs in the Indian and Pacific Oceans as far north as Hawaii. They hunt fish, such as snappers, damselfish and eels, as well as octopus, lobsters and crabs. Whitetip reef sharks compete with other reef sharks for food.

Some parts of the ocean, such as reefs, are full of different types of life. Many large and small fish stay close to coral reefs to keep out of the reach of sharks.

MEET THE SHARKS

Great white sharks and whitetip reef sharks are among the best-known and fiercest sharks, but they are not alone. More than 400 species of shark prowl the oceans. They range from huge 12-metre- (40-foot-) long whale sharks to tiny spined pygmy sharks no more than 20 centimetres (8 inches) long!

Although sharks are a type of fish, they are quite different in some ways. Most fish have skeletons made of bones, but sharks have skeletons made of a flexible substance called cartilage. Most fish have scales, while sharks have a rough skin.

A lemon shark is one of the smaller types of shark. It grows to around 3 metres (10 feet) long. It is called a lemon shark because its skin can look yellow, like a lemon.

LINKS IN THE FOOD CHAIN

Not all sharks are fierce predators. Whale sharks and basking sharks feed only on plankton and small sea animals. These sharks have huge mouths that take in large amounts of seawater. As the water is pushed through the sharks' special gills, tiny animals become trapped.

A whale shark swims with its huge mouth wide open. Unlike most sharks, it has no teeth. It feeds on plankton, the smallest form of life in the ocean.

TOP PREDATOR

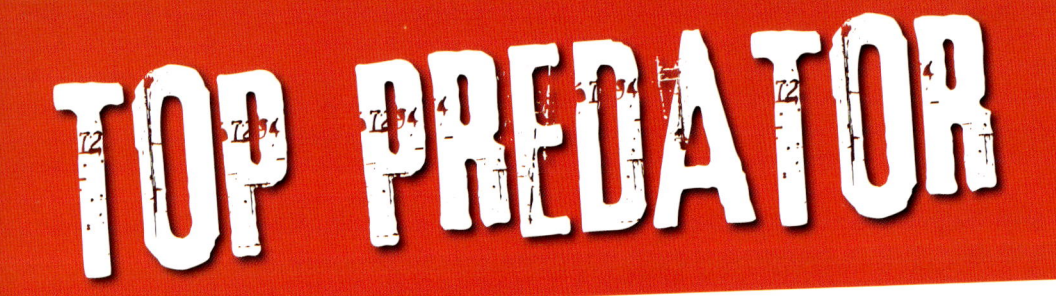

Almost everything about a shark makes it a super killer. Its body is designed for speed. Many sharks can swim at up to 32 kilometres (20 miles) per hour and mako sharks are even faster. When a shark catches its prey, its strong jaws and sharp teeth rip the animal apart.

In spite of their speed and jaws, sharks would not be successful hunters without their incredible senses. They can hear and smell their prey from far away. They even have a special sense, which gives them the ability to "feel" the electrical signals given out by prey.

A shark is a well-designed killing machine that brings terror wherever it goes.

A great white shark is one of the most dangerous of all sharks. It grows up to 6 metres (20 feet) long and hunts tuna, dolphins and other sea animals.

KILLER FACT

Small sharks can be as fierce as large ones. Cookiecutter sharks are less than 60 centimetres (2 feet) long, but they attack almost anything. They have incredibly sharp teeth and take bites out of whales, seals and tuna. They also eat squid as large as themselves.

SHARK ATTACK

A shark attack can begin when the prey is still very far away. Sounds travel fast in water, so the shark may hear the animal even before it smells it. As the prey moves, the shark listens for the very low sounds it makes and follows it.

As the shark closes in, it uses its fins to manoeuvre around its prey. Then it attacks! The shark moves so quickly it usually takes its prey by surprise. Large sharks often kill their prey instantly. If the unlucky animal struggles, however, the noise of its splashing soon attracts other sharks. They then all join the attack.

KILLER FACT

Sharks can often get close to their prey without being spotted because most sharks are camouflaged. Tiger sharks, for example, have a light-coloured belly, so they blend with the sky when they are seen from below. Their dark back, however, makes them difficult to see from above.

This shark has attacked, but its prey is fighting back! Before long, more sharks will arrive to join the action.

Although the water is clear, this tiger shark's belly is well camouflaged against the sky above.

STREAMLINING

A shark streaks through the water at great speed. It is streamlined like many fish and moves its tail from side to side to propel itself forward. The shark's long body is covered with strong muscles. The muscles make the tail lash to power the shark through the water.

Streamlining helps the shark to move fast. Its pointed snout and torpedo-shaped body cut cleanly through the water. The more streamlined the shark's shape, the less the water resists it and the faster the shark moves. Even the shark's skin helps to reduce friction. Instead of the large scales that many fish have, a shark's skin is covered with tiny scales that help the water flow over it.

A blue shark is quite lazy, but it can swim quickly when it needs to. Its extra-long tail and side fins help it to slice through the water.

LINKS IN THE FOOD CHAIN

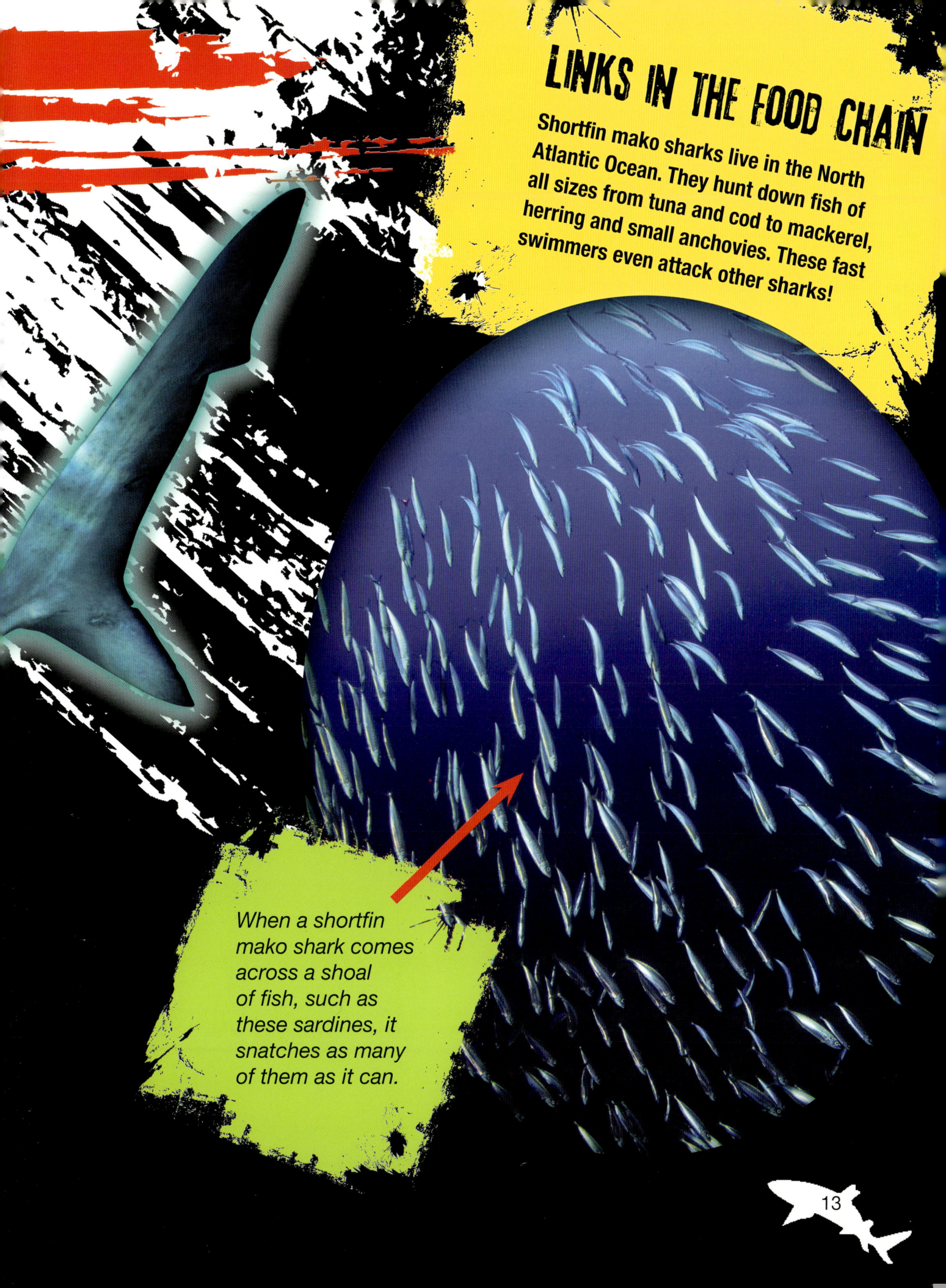

Shortfin mako sharks live in the North Atlantic Ocean. They hunt down fish of all sizes from tuna and cod to mackerel, herring and small anchovies. These fast swimmers even attack other sharks!

When a shortfin mako shark comes across a shoal of fish, such as these sardines, it snatches as many of them as it can.

13

FANTASTIC FINS

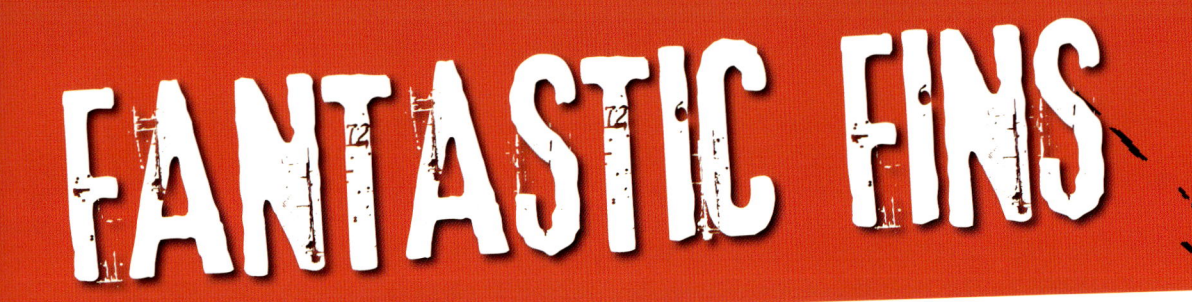

A shark not only swims forwards quickly, it can also stop and turn faster than its prey. The shark's fins help it to twist and turn. They allow the shark to get into a good position above its prey before attacking.

A shark has a large fin in the middle of its back, called the dorsal fin. It may also have smaller fins near its tail. These fins allow it to steer and stay level in the water. A shark also has fins on its sides, which it uses a bit like the wings of an aeroplane. It tilts them up and down to move upwards and downwards.

A blacktip shark can twist and turn its head sharply to catch a fish.

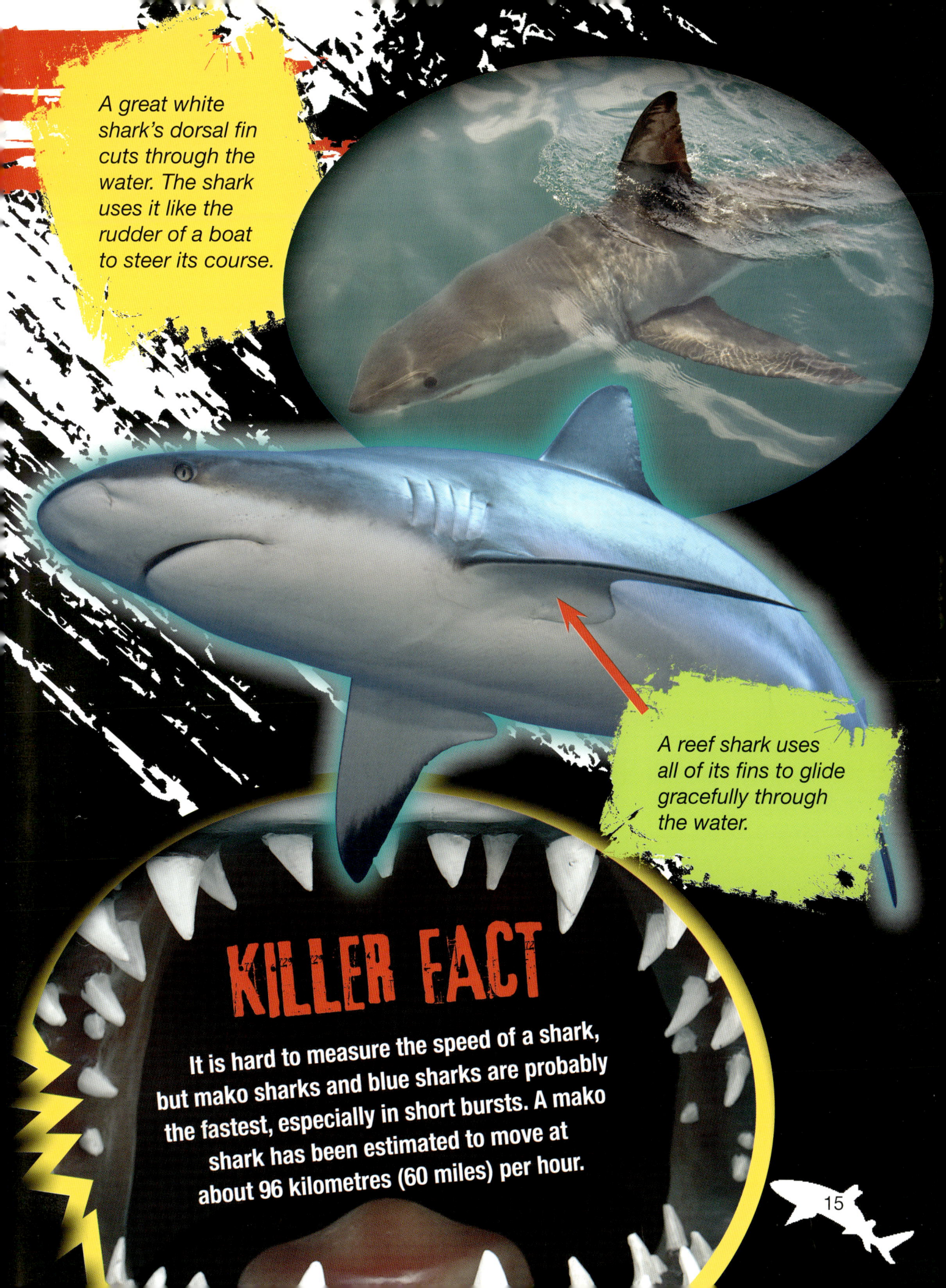

A great white shark's dorsal fin cuts through the water. The shark uses it like the rudder of a boat to steer its course.

A reef shark uses all of its fins to glide gracefully through the water.

KILLER FACT

It is hard to measure the speed of a shark, but mako sharks and blue sharks are probably the fastest, especially in short bursts. A mako shark has been estimated to move at about 96 kilometres (60 miles) per hour.

KILLER TEETH

A shark's most dangerous weapons are its powerful jaws and sharp teeth. Its mouth is on the underside of its head, so when the shark reaches its prey, it slows down and lifts its snout. It then pushes its mouth forwards and opens its jaws.

With larger prey, the shark clamps its jaws around part of the body and rips off a mouthful of flesh. It swallows smaller fish whole. Tiger sharks have jagged teeth, which slice through flesh and bones, like a chainsaw. Large tiger sharks can crush the tough shells of sea turtles.

This lemon shark is bearing its fearsome teeth as it joins in a feeding frenzy.

A shark opens its mouth, ready to grab its prey.

Like most sharks, great white sharks have a never-ending supply of sharp teeth.

KILLER FACT

A shark has up to 3,000 razor-sharp teeth. They are arranged in its mouth in several rows. When a tooth falls out, another moves forward to take its place. New teeth just keep on growing. A shark can have up to 50,000 teeth in its lifetime!

AMAZING SMELL

A shark needs all of its senses to be a top predator, but it depends most of all on its sense of smell. A shark's sense of smell is 10,000 times better than a human's. It can sense blood and other animal smells in the water from miles away.

A shark has two nostrils, one on each side of its snout. As the shark swims along, water flows through its nostrils. A shark can tell which direction a smell is coming from, because its nostrils work separately from each other. If a smell reaches one nostril before the other, the shark knows that the smell must be coming from that side.

A shark's nostrils are below its eyes and above its mouth.

KILLER FACT

Sharks are especially attracted to the smell of blood and to smells made by injured or frightened animals. It is said that a shark can smell a teaspoon of blood in the water in an Olympic-sized swimming pool!

An Olympic swimming pool is just under 50 metres (165 feet) long, but if a shark was swimming in it, it could smell a few drops of blood anywhere in the water.

SPECIAL EYESIGHT

Sharks use their senses of smell and hearing to track down prey. When they swim within around 9–15 metres (30–50 feet) of their prey, their sense of sight takes over. Sharks can see well in the dark. This is useful because they often hunt at night or in deep, dark water.

Only the water near the surface of the sea is well lit, so a shark's eyes are designed to work well in dim light. Like cats, sharks have a special layer of cells that reflect light to make it brighter. Their eyes also contain more of the type of cells that see in dim light.

A shark has an extra see-through eyelid on its eye. The shark closes it to protect its eye when it attacks its prey.

20

LINKS IN THE FOOD CHAIN

Dogfish are a type of small shark, which eat many different types of prey. Spiny dogfish are a type of dogfish that live off the east coast of North America. They feed on lots of sea creatures, including cod, haddock and herring, as well as crabs, jellyfish, squid and octopus.

A hammerhead shark has a broad snout with an eye at each end. Together, the eyes allow the shark to see all around and above and below.

OTHER SENSES

A shark has two unique senses, which help it to sense when another animal is close by. A tube called the lateral line runs under the skin along each side of the shark's body. The tube is filled with water, which moves when the water around the shark moves.

All living things create a flow of weak electricity. Special cells in the skin on a shark's head detect this electricity, and allow the shark to "see" prey hidden on the seabed. Earth is surrounded by an electrical field, so the cells on a shark's head may also act like a compass, helping the shark to find its way in the ocean.

The wobbegong shark is well camouflaged against the seabed. Its jaws are covered with feelers called barbs, which it uses to search for prey in the sand.

KILLER FACT

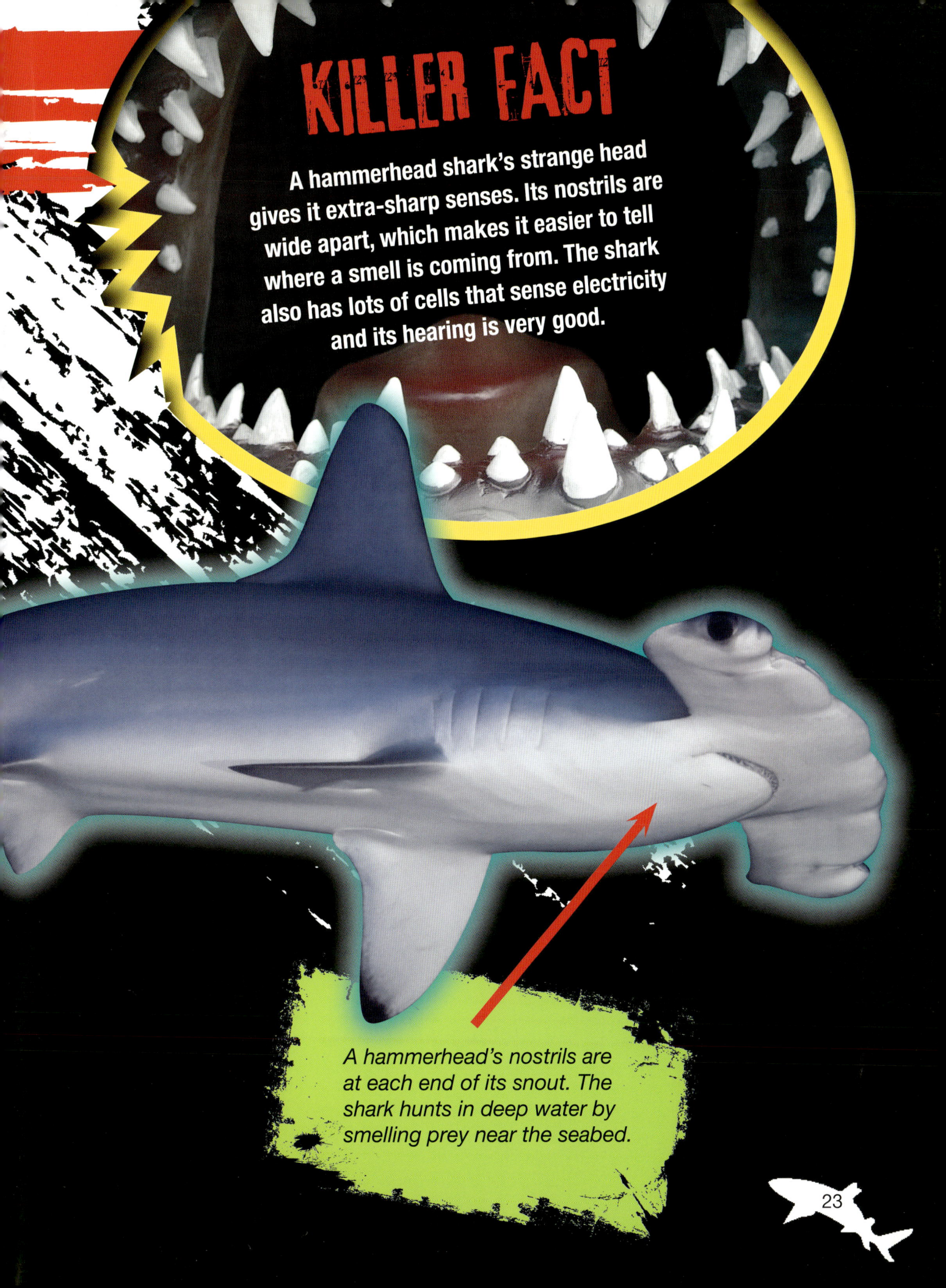

A hammerhead shark's strange head gives it extra-sharp senses. Its nostrils are wide apart, which makes it easier to tell where a smell is coming from. The shark also has lots of cells that sense electricity and its hearing is very good.

A hammerhead's nostrils are at each end of its snout. The shark hunts in deep water by smelling prey near the seabed.

GREAT SURVIVOR

Sharks are ancient creatures. They have been hunting in the oceans for hundreds of millions of years. People have found shark teeth that are 420 million years old! At that time, few plants or animals lived on land, but the oceans swarmed with life, including a type of small shark called *Cladoselache*.

Cladoselache was only about 1.8 metres (6 feet) long, but it was a fast swimmer. It died out around 350 million years ago. Modern sharks began to prowl the oceans about 100 million years ago. Megalodon, the largest shark that has ever lived, was among one of the first modern sharks.

This fossil is of the gaping mouth of a shark that lived more than 2 million years ago.

KILLER FACT

Megalodon lived from 36 to 1.8 million years ago and was an incredible 15 metres (50 feet) or more long. Its teeth were up to 17 centimetres (7 inches) long and were shaped like those of a great white shark. Megalodon hunted whales and large turtles.

The huge size of a megalodon's tooth suggests that this ancient shark was more than twice as long as a great white shark.

Great white sharks have ruled in the oceans for 16 million years.

25

SHARK DANGERS

Although sharks have survived for hundreds of millions of years, they are now threatened as never before. The number of sharks in the northwest Atlantic Ocean was cut in half between 1986 and 2000. Several species of shark are in danger of dying out. What is happening to sharks?

Humans are the main danger to sharks. Fishing is destroying many types of sharks. Sharks are often caught accidentally on the long lines used by fishing trawlers. Many sharks are also caught deliberately, because their fins are so valuable. In China, shark fin soup used to be a luxury, served only to the emperor. Now it is popular with wealthy people in China and around the world.

Great white sharks are hunted by using bait at the end of a strong fishing line.

KILLER FACT

People are terrified of being attacked by sharks, but shark attacks are very unusual. While humans kill around 40 million sharks a year, only an average of five people are killed by sharks each year.

These baby sharks are being sold as food in a fish market in Dubai, in the United Arab Emirates.

These dried shark fins are on sale in a traditional Chinese shop. Shark fins sell for around £280 per pound.

NO MORE SHARKS?

What happens when sharks disappear from the top of the food chain? You may think that fish and other sea animals below them would thrive if sharks disappeared. This is what some fishermen and scientists thought, but they were wrong. When sharks disappear, animals lower down the food chain suffer too.

Sharks help to keep the food chain in balance so that every species has enough food to survive. When large sharks disappear, the fish and other animals they fed on increase in number. These extra fish soon wipe out the animals they prey on, which is why we need the shark to stay at the top of its food chain!

A shark usually targets old, sick and slow fish. This leaves the healthier, fast fish free to breed, which makes the overall fish population stronger.

28

LINKS IN THE FOOD CHAIN

Hammerhead sharks and bull sharks once preyed on rays and other fish off the east coast of North America. When these large sharks disappeared, fishermen found that their catches of shellfish disappeared too. With the sharks gone, the shellfish had all been eaten by the rays!

Cownose rays love to eat scallops. When barriers were put up to protect scallops from these rays in the northeast United States, the scallops thrived again.

GLOSSARY

camouflaged hard to see because the colouring blends into the surroundings

cartilage rubbery material that is tough and strong, but softer than bone

cells the smallest units of life. Each cell in a living thing has a job to do.

chainsaw saw that is driven by an electric engine and cuts through objects very fast

compass instrument that uses the magnetism of Earth to show the direction of north

dorsal related to the back. A shark's dorsal fin is on its back.

fins flat parts of a fish or shark that are attached to its main body

food chain way in which one animal feeds on another animal in a chain that ends with plants. Energy from the sun and the plants pass up the food chain.

friction force that occurs when an object moves across another object or through liquid or air

gills parts of a fish or shark that take in oxygen from the water as it passes through them

lateral lines lines of small canals along the sides of fish that can sense movement

manoeuvre use skill to move into a better position

nostrils openings on an animal's face through which it smells

plankton tiny plants and animals that float on the surface of water. Plankton are so small they can only be seen through a microscope.

predators animals that hunt other animals for food

prey animals that are hunted by other animals for food

scales hard, flat discs that protect the skin of some animals, such as bony fish

senses parts of the body that detect particular things in the environment, such as light, chemicals and sound waves. The senses give a living thing information about the world around it.

species group of living things that are so similar they can produce offspring

streamlined smooth, curved shape that moves fast and easily through a liquid or air

FIND OUT MORE

Shark (Eyewitness), DK (DK Children, 2014)

Shark vs. Killer Whale (Animal Rivals), Isabel Thomas (Raintree, 2017)

Sharks (Go! Field Guide), Scholastic (Scholastic, 2019)

Sharks and Other Deadly Ocean Creatures, DK (DK Children, 2016)

The Ultimate Book of Sharks (Ultimate), Brian Skerry (National Geographic Kids, 2018)

WEBSITES

The National Geographic Kids website has fun facts on the great white shark:
www.natgeokids.com/uk/discover/animals/sea-life/great-white-sharks/

Check out the DK website for lots of information on sharks:
www.dkfindout.com/uk/animals-and-nature/fish/sharks/

The CBBC Shark Bites site has lots of videos of Steve Backshall exploring different types of sharks:
www.bbc.co.uk/cbbc/shows/shark-bites

INDEX

ancient sharks 24–25

basking sharks 7
blacktip sharks 14
blood 18–19
blue sharks 12, 15

camouflage 10–11, 22
cartilage 6

dogfish 21

fins 10, 12, 14–15, 26–27
fishing 26
food chains 4–5, 7, 21, 28–29

great white sharks 6, 9, 15, 17, 25–26

hammerhead sharks 21, 23, 29
hunting 4–5, 8–9, 13, 16, 23, 25

lemon sharks 6, 16

mako sharks 8, 13, 15
megalodon 24–25

prey 4–5, 7–10, 13–14, 16, 23, 25

reef sharks 4–5, 15

senses 8, 10, 18–23
shark attacks 10–11, 14, 16, 20, 27
speed 8, 10, 12–15
spined pygmy sharks 6
streamlined bodies 12–13

teeth 8–9, 16–17, 24–25
tiger sharks 10–11, 16

whale sharks 6–7
whitetip reef sharks 4–6
wobbegong sharks 22